the
love
i do
to you

MARIAH WHELAN

POETRY

 **EYEWEAR** PUBLISHING

First published in 2019
by Eyewear Publishing Ltd
Suite 333, 19-21 Crawford Street
Marylebone, London W1H 1PJ
United Kingdom

Cover design and typeset by Edwin Smet
Printed in England by TJ International Ltd, Padstow, Cornwall

ISBN 978-1-912477-87-6

WWW.EYEWEARPUBLISHING.COM

For the women in my life who saved me,
including myself.

Mariah Whelan
is a poet from Oxford, UK.
Her poems appear in *The Aesthetica Creative
Writing Annual 2019*, *Best New British and Irish Poets 2018*, *The
Poetry Book Society* website, *The Interpreter's House* and elsewhere.
Her writing has been longlisted for The Rialto and RSPB
Nature and Place Poetry Prize, shortlisted for The PBS Student
Poetry Prize, The Bridport Prize, The Melita Hume Prize and
won The AM Heath Prize. Mariah has degrees from Queen's
University Belfast and The University of Oxford and she
currently holds a PhD research scholarship at The University
of Manchester where she is writing a new collection of poems
and researching trauma and representation in contemporary
Irish fiction. She is one of the lead creative practitioners in
the interdisciplinary 'Truth Tellers' project, a creative-critical
collaboration bringing together art and International Relations
methodologies funded by King's College, London. Outside of
her writing and research Mariah is Director of Oxford Writers'
House, a hub that brings Oxford's universities and local
community into dialogue through creative writing projects.

TABLE OF CONTENTS

Part One

City of Rivers

Winter

Map of Newcastle upon Tyne

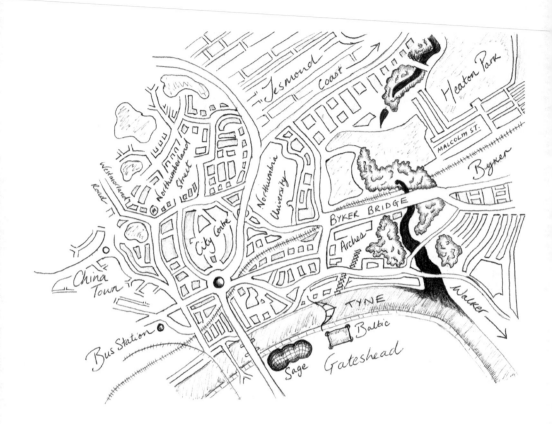

THE COACH STATION, ST JAMES BOULEVARD, NEWCASTLE UPON TYNE

Bright station and all around soft dark.
Toothpaste and sleep, coffee and the white crunch
of salt on the concourse. The headlamps snorting –
boarding as the first gull caws began to ricochet.

That's how it was the morning I left.
Too cold for snow, the hills thick with February
sloped black-backed and low to where the Tyne
bloomed in the wake of a boat.

I was less going somewhere than getting out,
away from the terraces and rain, the tower blocks,
the yellow Metro stops that took me in loops,
out into the waking-up day.

But mostly I was getting away from you.
The river below breathing as all rivers do.

She

52 MALCOLM STREET,
NEWCASTLE UPON TYNE

I tried to get back to the beginning:
I had a girlfriend then suddenly didn't
and it had something to do with you and how
I always knew where you were, could find you.

At parties, I mean
or at a club, in the library
I could feel my way along the atoms
to find the seat next to yours.

Slipping inside you was a homecoming.
All your knowledge and goodness,
your body on top, heart underneath
and the way it beat in my hands.

But your soul (be fair now)
I never really asked for that.

He

THE AIRPORT INDUSTRIAL ESTATE, NEWCASTLE UPON TYNE

During the week I had work:
£400 every Friday for tea-making and invoices,
for filing and being the only one who knew
how to fix the website.

£400 for making sure the boss had tea
ready and waiting. Holding his mug as he changed,
for while he'd do guttering and de-mould walls
he specialised in inspecting tenants out of bonds.

'It's good money and not forever,' I said.
You were playing guitar, nodding while I changed,
getting ready to go out. I flipped over my hair
to brush the kinks and when I stood you were gone.

Yes, there are questions we ask with our mouths,
more we ask with hands, thigh bones, hearts.

She

52 MALCOLM STREET, HEATON, NEWCASTLE UPON TYNE

Rain. Not much of a morning. Descaled the kettle
with an old spoon and watched Jeremy Kyle.
I did the crossword and pulled out *Guardian* centrefolds,
collaging the wall in giant pandas, Afghan women in blue.

You wouldn't be home for hours. I rolled a joint,
smoked it out the kitchen door and slowly the house
unravelled: open doors, sleepy eyes asking me
for, 'Seconds on that one, mate.'

Between smokes I stood and watched the drizzle,
the blades of puddle in the yard filling with clouds, gulls.
Later I would restring my bass, find the speakers
but first: toast and a drink of water.

I'd need more tobacco soon.
Rain. Not much of a day.

He

52 MALCOLM STREET, HEATON, NEWCASTLE UPON TYNE

'We used to take the Yama-note line round and around
totally high. Freak out salary-men on their way to work.'
My friend Max and I were in the kitchen drinking tea,
talking about his year in Japan. 'Freedom,' he laughed —

'or as close as you can get to it.
I was an eye invisible in steam and city,
light, liquor and money. How much
money are you making here?'

And then, you opened the door and came in
tramping puddle-muck on your way
to the living room. 'Fucking white people,' Max said.
'Who the fuck wears shoes indoors?'

I didn't know if I was allowed to or should answer.
My cheeks grew hot, burned.

She

THE ARCHES STUDIOS, BYKER, NEWCASTLE UPON TYNE

A sizzle of white paper then smoke
billowing, the cigarette red in the gloom.
I ran my fingers through my hair,
adjusted the strap, checked she was still in tune.

We'd played all night: jammed,
locked down riffs, recorded bits and played them back,
the weed making it flow,
feeling my way, know when to kick in, cut back.

'Stay a bit longer, man,' someone said.
I looked at my watch: nearly light outside.
'Nah,' he smiled. 'Leave the bass and let's just
chill.' I thought about you asleep in our bed,

how I needed these demos done.
'Aye, alright,' I said.

He

52 MALCOLM STREET, HEATON, NEWCASTLE UPON TYNE

Max, I was pretty sure, was gay. Who he'd been before
was locked tight as a shell. Family, friends, his childhood
were pieces of grit calcifying away from me as we sat,
all of us out at a party, Max rigid as a hare at my side.

Getting him drunk didn't help. The one time you got him stoned
we had to pull him out of hedges, giggling the whole way home.
'I think Max is gay,' I said. 'So what?' you whispered,
turning off his light, closing his bedroom door.

That night I lay in bed and thought about how it felt
to live my life. Like it was a clean room and you
kept coming in, messing it up, not using a coaster
when once I didn't mind if you came in with dirty shoes.

'Hey,' I said. 'I can't sleep.'
You just rolled towards me, pulled me under the sheets.

She

52 MALCOLM STREET, HEATON, NEWCASTLE UPON TYNE

When I was three, Dad took us out to see the shoals
glittering off Warrenpoint. I remember the rhythms
of the water, peering into the grey sea, the cruel way
they left the catch to die, each scale a prism.

Back on shore he told me, 'Keep one, son,' trawled
a blade through its gills, the sun a chrism on the open
wound. Even though I was so small I knew
I couldn't cry: my lips went numb with biting.

When we made love, I dipped my head in memory.
Held tight, trying to concentrate on pillowcase, sheet-seams,
fish limbs flat against the dock, trying to control myself,
haul our small boat across the fathoms.

I didn't know what you needed. Whatever it was
for the love of God, I wished you'd take it.

He

BLYTH VALLEY, NORTHUMBERLAND

We took the coast road as far as Willington and turned north,
drove until the carriageways filtered to a single track, a bend
blinded by uncut hedge. He eased the car into a blue valley,
river-bottomed, full of mists rising to meet us through the reeds.

He cut the engine and silence settled in: tyres on the gravel,
cows rubbing against a gate, their breath whitening
into the spread of milky way, an arch of frost
over the roses, breathing softly.

'Hey,' I said. 'Let's keep going.' On the gear-stick Max's hand
contracted, eased into first, accelerated into the grey moor
above the village. Under the stone bridge the water sparkled,
rushed into the who-knows-what dark dream of its bend –

moving I felt clean, was foam.
I felt free, finally home.

She

OUSEBURN, BELOW BYKER BRIDGE, NEWCASTLE UPON TYNE

'This place has always been a lung,' you'd said,
stroking your soft fingers over my cheek.
'Gauze to mop up smog, catch from the slums
the tubercular hack of ship yards, the coal face.'

The cold sound of the city whipped across the burn:
I was walking to the practice rooms with my bass strapped tight
breasting the pour of a gale, your words like trolleys
half-submerged in the river-clay and weeds.

I'd found the advert slipped between the pages
of your latest book: *Japan,* it said, *Teach English.*
I tucked it back and sat for a while, then took the stairs
two at a time to the river: the cold breeze, the air

thick with memories, white touches –
fingers of ice that left my cheek tingling.

He

BYKER BRIDGE, BYKER, NEWCASTLE UPON TYNE

When I was twelve they showed a bit about a man
who jumped from Howsgill Bridge. It was tea-time,
fish fingers in front of the TV and the man they'd sent
to fix the fence insisting, 'He was there, then gone.'

I saw him in my head for weeks, his arms a perfect V
wanting not his death but something of his falling.
'*Japan*.' I whispered and let the word drop into the Ouse,
caught by the hogweed flowering and deflowering in the wind.

'I thought you'd be interested,' Max had said. 'You don't seem
the sort of person who... you know.' I shook my head.
'The sort of person who ends up here, wasting their life
on a man like him.' I told him to mind his own business.

But it was still there: the job ad he gave me.
Japan I whispered, holding it tight.

She

CONNAUGHT MEWS, JESMOND, NEWCASTLE UPON TYNE

'I'd go for it,' Max said, stirring
sugar into his tea. You were running late at work
leaving us alone, awkwardly staring
at light going gold on the kitchen floor.

'If you made enough she could give up that job,
wouldn't have to support you.' 'Support me?' Max gave a shrug.
'Or whatever it is you do.' And that was that,
twenty minutes later we were outside the flat, my heart pumping blood.

'Hiya,' the girl said. 'Come in but it's shoes off I'm afraid.'
Pale-white plaster, wrought iron and bay trees,
classical music on low. 'Now, like I said, everything I sell's fair trade.
Just me,' she smiled. 'And my Chem. Eng. degree.'

The white powder and bags sat packaged by some scales:
'Cash only,' she smiled. 'For these smaller sales.'

He

WESTMORLAND ROAD, NEWCASTLE UPON TYNE

Bright city and all around rivering dark.
Through closed eyes I saw mud recrusting
on the diesel-flats, bends and bridges
arching over the Tyne, alleys I'd never walk at night.

Inside, the party pressed itself against the glass –
three storeys of smoke and camo-nets, pink light slashing
into the street. It always took me by surprise: spring
like a sudden miracle, nights warm enough to sit outside.

But then a taxi cab pulled over. Inside was a woman,
about my age who, stumbling and bent double, sent
a stream of curry-coloured vomit spattering across the street,
steaming where it ran in rivulets across the path.

I closed my eyes and felt the waste of it all
wash over me. I needed you to come through this time.

She

WESTMORLAND ROAD, NEWCASTLE UPON TYNE

I remember when you first said you loved me.
Above all else it was so fucking cool,
'I know it's too soon,' you said, zipping your jeans.
'But whatever, I just do.'

How violently the crowd reeled
when the music cut. Lights flashed,
smoke swirled and bodies
spun to face the decks.

Across the room I watched you dance
with Max. After everything, I'd ended up
with nothing. My band took some on the tick
then he took a cut I didn't even know I owed.

'You know,' he grinned. 'Seeing how I fronted cash.'
You found me with nothing, exactly what I always had.

He

Part Two
広島
Wide Island
Spring

Map of Hiroshima

MT. SOKO, HIROSHIMA, JAPAN

All morning we followed the trail past hare-runs and paths left
by rutting tanuki. Up, until the air iced our cheeks, glazed the rocks
in mercurial dew, a corset of cool that laced the loosening ferns
in silver. Up, until we turned a bend and stumbled into light.

Hiroshima lay below us like a toy: tin cars turned
down miniature roads, tree-lined avenues, patches of park –
the blocks marked with a tower, billboard, or temple. Smoke
curled under awnings, rivers forked and boats broke

the rust-coloured water where, beachless, the bay dropped off.
'Nothing between it and America,' someone said. 'Save Hawaii,'
and the million islets of the inland sea piercing the horizon,
making the date-line gauzy with fog.

'Well, this is it.' someone said.
'The best view in Hiroshima. Welcome home.'

She

52 MALCOLM STREET, HEATON, NEWCASTLE UPON TYNE

It was the first summer you came to stay on my parents' farm,
the sky still aquarium-coloured at midnight, all stars and borealis.
'No,' you said to me. 'That's Venus,' lighting the yard,
the tractor, the cow-sheds and the bog-land beyond.

'See that there?' I said, pointing from the peat fields
to the pines up by The Long Mountain. 'All that's ours.'
We climbed onto the roof and lay watching the sky,
listened to the birds and fields sleepless with midsummer.

When I woke from the dream, the girl's feet still felt
like yours. I lay there naked and hungover,
touching my toes to hers until she woke,
said, 'Good morning,' and kissed me.

Afterwards I checked my email:
no new messages received.

He

YOKOGAWA, HIROSHIMA, JAPAN

'I mean, yes, *technically* I'm from Texas but, like, I lived in France.'
Kristen and I were riding across town to Lopez's restaurant.
Left on the Johoku bridge, down an underpass, our bike spokes clacking
in the wind, up onto the pavement past the station.

Inside, water and fat vaporised where they touched the teppan grill.
Pork flesh sizzled, eggs cracked and noodles went kinetic with heat,
'I –' Kristen took a long pause. 'Have missed this shit.'
My new friend threw cusses like they were Keats, raised her beer and said,

'So tell me, are you running away or just lost?' 'Pardon?'
'We're all one or the other,' she laughed. 'And I like you,
let's get it out of the way.' 'Well which one are you?' I shot back
and she smiled, spooning noodles and cheese up to her mouth.

Afterwards we stopped by the castle. 'Come on,' she said.
'Let's dump the bikes and get a drink at Shack.'

She

THE ARCHES STUDIO, HEATON, NEWCASTLE UPON TYNE

'Mate,' one of the lads said. 'This is getting ridiculous.'
Overhead a train rattled across the bridge.
 'You can't wait forever, just in case she comes back.'
I was sat stringing my bass: 'Aye,' I said. 'You're right.'

'What you doing?' he said, looking panicked.
'I didn't mean now.' But I'd already put the guitar down,
reached for the soft cover and my coat –
 'Nah, mate. You're right. I can't do this anymore.'

I felt sick rising as I googled *teach English abroad,*
hit return and waited as the links piled up.
I picked my site and began filling out:
name, sex, age and clicked *attach CV –*

I'd show you who I was. How I could be
much more than what you needed.

He

NAGAREKAWA, HIROSHIMA, JAPAN

'But that was all before I came here,' the boy said.
Irish, like you. My age. Skinny with a lovely way of pulling
on his peaked cap. I smiled and offered him a cigarette —
'I should buy some of my own. I'll be back in, like, less than five?'

I watched him disappear between the cabs that stretched
along the street, under archways strung with silver streamers,
neon signs, a hundred doorways leading off, some concrete,
others cloth-covered, salt and bottled water to purify the lintels.

The strange thing was that right below I thought I'd seen a Family Mart
full of salary men swigging chu-hai. Aisles brilliant with the kimono
of hostess girls, teenagers buying Pianissimo Pêche and Marlboro Reds.
No matter, I thought. I laughed at my mistake.

Ten minutes passed then ten minutes more.
My whisky paling, melt-water beading my glass.

She

NORTHUMBERLAND STREET, NEWCASTLE UPON TYNE

'You got any drugs on you, son?' the fat one said, arching into the back.
'I'm not g'arrest ya, like,' he twisted around further. 'We're off at two.'
Shoppers buffeted the panda car, popping umbrellas as my heart beat
electric, trying to decide to trust him, hand over what was in my shoe.

There had been this continental market up Grey Street,
I didn't intend to take something, was halfway down
when the store-cop got hold of my shoulder,
spun me round and said, 'Gotcha, you little shit.'

They seemed to find it funny. The fat one's stab-vest shook
as he said, 'that's hardly worth admittin'!' Slapped the driver,
took the bag of green, wound the window and let the air suck
it out, 'I'm not doing any bloody paperwork for *that!*'

I laughed too, as they delivered me to the charge desk
until I read, upside down, the sergeant scribbling *charges pressed*.

He

HONDORI SHOPPING MALL, HIROSHIMA, JAPAN

'Well, I'm not exactly sure what you thought was going to happen, babe.'
Kristen frowned. 'There's a reason my major erotic relationship is with cheese.
Foreign guys, I'm sorry, but they're in Japan to get with ladies who are Japanese.'
She began to fiddle with a bin of ketai chains, not meeting my eye.

There had been more whisky. I'd cycled home with no shoes,
cruised past the salary-men sleeping it off in flower beds.
'Make sure you eat a lot of oily fish,' Kristen said, looking me up
and down. 'Not having sex is super bad for your knees.'

I didn't mention getting home. How, once I found my keys
I sat and cried on my futon, decided I needed to hear your voice.
The click of the line connecting, the pause full of static before the ringing
came clean, loud and I left you the world's most expensive voicemail.

I remembered the taste of mint and the bathroom mirror.
Picking mascara off with my finger, then black.

She

52 MALCOLM STREET, HEATON, NEWCASTLE UPON TYNE

The envelope hit the mat with a thud,
heavy in a slippery spill of Co-op ads.
Under *convictions* it read *none* –
I carried it into the light:

Korean visas, it seemed, didn't care about cautions.
'Thank fuck,' I breathed and felt the air go sliding
out the door. Later I sat, trying to imagine
how it would be, when I heard my phone upstairs.

When I reached it they were gone, the voicemail icon
visible on the lock screen. I stared at the cassette,
the blank space where the number usually was
empty, the caller not recognised.

'Hello there,' a voice said as I dialled.
'Please top-up to make the call required.'

He

渋 谷
Bitter Valley
Summer

Map of Shibuya

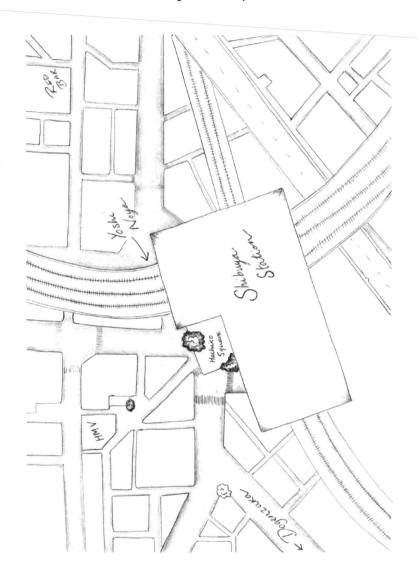

SHIBUYA STATION, TOKYO

'Did I ever tell you 'bout the time I nearly had a threesome?'
Kristen and I were on the bullet train, threading miles
like they were pearls on a string. 'That happened in Tokyo.
French couple. That city, it's just... well, you'll see.'

We followed the crowd like we knew where we were going,
shoaling over Hachikō Square till it thinned and settled
like bubbles in lemonade. Hot rain fell in soft, fat drops
that plucked at the lights reflected in the puddles.

I had thought I would feel the way a bee must, deep in its wax core.
A single cell in a million, finally free in neon lights,
hot traffic and bodies. Instead, I only felt the pressure
of my backpack, couldn't look up, wished you were there.

I felt like an ocean who knows it's not a wave
but feels it passing through her all the same.

She

SEOUL TO SUNCHEON HIGHWAY, SOUTH KOREA

There were no stars in Seoul. Instead, through buffed arrival halls
and the automatic airport doors, the city melted in. Lights
wove canopies six storeys high, shrunk the city, hid the sky,
narrowed the streets to a stall-sized glow.

Horns, brakes, tyres: the neon sound of Gangnam-gu came clear
through the wound-down windows. At the station I changed,
clutching the printed address more precious than a passport:
'Suncheon,' the principal told me, 'like truncheon.'

Rocked into a six-hour sleep I dreamed of you, again.
We were nineteen, mooching in the Baltic, it was dark at four
but inside it was darker, the exhibition a cave
of birds singing from human lips on vid screens.

I saw the hundred mouths and felt your hand holding mine
and I knew, this time, things would be different.

He

TSUKIJI FISH MARKET, HARUMI STREET, TOKYO

The last tuna lay on a wooden slat, dead. Silver belly split,
his curves an arch corrugated in snow. The meat hissed
with cold, the ridged place where the gills once were stuffed
with tarpaulin, his head and lunate tail removed.

The channels were thick with venous slurry. Our feet disturbing
the hot froth of blood, bleach and steam escaping from bodies.
There were buckets of octopuses still alive, eels elvering
to catch what the fish-mongers' knives sent flying.

We were desperate to show we weren't tourists.
Stiffened when an American man reached to touch the tuna –
'Bakka,' Kristen hissed, meaning stupid. The chef looked up,
laughed and reached across the stall with two fresh pieces.

They wobbled on the blade, gelatinous with fish stink.
'Eat,' he said, the trails of connective tissue dangling.

She

HEART ENGLISH ACADEMY, JORE-DONG, SUNCHEON, SOUTH KOREA

The pink cross hovered over the path, oddly neon
as I walked to work. It went in and out of view,
disappeared behind the guts of half-demolished houses,
a Mini Stop, broken fences, old telegraph poles and tarps.

The church itself was downtown, obscured by balconies
and faded karaoke signs. Dust blew in from the highway
and on the corner a teenage girl sold kimchi
next to old men, their chat rough as engines.

But from my bedroom window, I'd seen another world.
In the dark I'd felt the black weight of a mountain
and woke to see a wall of green where mist and fog made
the peak obscure, teeming with crickets and birds.

The principal announced herself without a knock.
'Hello,' she said. 'My name is Mrs Lee.'

He

DOGENZAKA (LOVE HOTEL HILL) SHIBUYA, TOKYO

With a vinyl clatter the phone by the bed exploded.
The man beside me rolled onto his arms, reached across
to lift the receiver. 'Hai, hai,' he said. 'Wakarimashita.'
Jeff, that was his name. I tried to stand and felt the world spin.

There had been the cool, clean taste of cocktails.
Rims crusted in salt, still on my lips as I kissed
the cricket-bat brown of his thigh. Now the room swam around me:
the mint-coloured floor, the wall tiles, the greening grout —

'We gotta go,' Jeff said. 'Who was that on the phone?' 'Look.'
He ran a hand through his hair. 'It's after two, we need to get out.
Come on,' he said and handed me my bra. The grey-scale lobby
smelled of old noodles and carpet cleaner. We passed the bodiless hand

that manned the frosted-glass front desk, out into the street
where I looked at this man, or rather his back, walking away.

She

SHEEDAE APARTMENTS, SUNCHEON, SOUTH KOREA

'It's pretty late,' she said. 'I should go.'
Around us the air cracked like stepped-on ice.
'Or we could get a beer, food – if you have the time.'
She seemed to hesitate. I noticed how smooth her skin was.

We pushed our bikes to Dong-cheon River
where she touched the rail and frowned as the water drifted
slow and slack, concrete from the mills silvering
its sickly surface until finally she said, 'Okay.'

I had no idea what I was doing as she handed me
battered somethings. Pointed out the gimbap,
blood-sausage, fresh river snail and chicken gizzards
in a spicy sauce that tasted of iron, hot fat.

'What's your first name, Mrs Lee?'
She smiled and said, 'My name's Yoon-mi.'

He

YOSHINOYA RESTAURANT, UNDERNEATH THE YAMANOTE TRACKS, SHIBUYA

Jeff traced a finger along the wet rim of his glass. He kept pouring
water, shooting little looks at the door, rearranging
his chopsticks. 'Well, I guess you'll probably need to get going.'
He wasn't a bad man. Barely five foot eight, a South Carolina drawl.

'Will you go straight to Hiroshima?' 'Probably.' 'You?'
'I gotta get ready for work, skype my sisters, boring stuff, really.'
When we said goodbye he gave me a business card,
and said, 'Well, as you Brits say, 'Cheerio!''

Hours before he'd been so tender: after Kristen disappeared,
leaving me alone in Red Bar. It was no bigger than a bedroom,
every inch of it covered in chandeliers and lamps with scarlet shades,
mirrors with gilt frames where he'd first appeared, smiling.

I hugged myself against the chill of the AC,
realised I'd left all my jewellery by the bed.

She

McCARTHY'S BAR, SUNCHEON, SOUTH KOREA

'There was a husband.' My friend and I were drinking Soju,
all we could afford before our end-of-month cheques cleared.
'They married young, he a student lawyer, she majoring
in French.' 'What happened?' 'I'll tell you if you get the beers.'

I brought back two bottles of Hite and filled his glass with froth.
'The problem was, four years later and she hadn't had a baby.
He and his Mom can't think why, drag her to a specialist who costs
a ton. Doctor says, 'She's on the pill, chump.''

Something twisted in my guts. I began to peel the label,
the cheap dyes staining my hands. 'Uh oh,' my friend said.
'You like her!' 'No, and if she's married it's hardly –'
'She's not married, dude. That Yoon-mi chick's divorced.'

It felt like the wind was suddenly behind me,
sunshine after months of dark.

He

반도
Peninsula
Autumn

Map of the Korean Peninsula and Japanese Archipelago

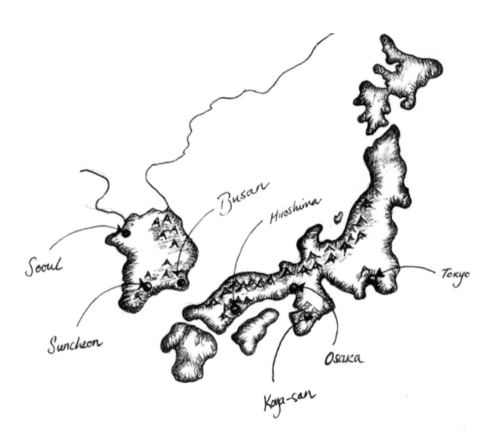

SHEEDAE APARTMENTS, SUNCHEON, SOUTH KOREA

All day rain was falling.
The ground was thick and clotted,
the trees grew heavy with their wet weight
until they toppled, shedding their crown of vines.

'Show me,' Yoon-mi said, 'more about your mountain.'
I could have told her how at night foxes darted
through the wood, how there were hillocked graves curving
to the south, earth that crumbled: fruited and dark.

'But it's more your mountain than mine,' I said. And it was true,
I was the foreigner, blind to the trees' braille.
'My love,' she said. 'What I care about knowing is you.'
On the trails some unknown animal called out,

the sound caught on my balcony: her neck, my lips –
our two bodies we couldn't escape.

He

FLIGHT KE784, 37° N, 131° E

'You mean the Yellow Sea,' you said and I heard a smile
spread across your face. I was telling you how our two countries
were once connected, my archipelago yoked to your peninsula.
'Don't say you've gone all colonial on me,' you smiled into the phone.

'It's the Japan Sea and everyone knows it,' I said. Rain
pounded my apartment windows, a Pacific-fuelled monsoon
or maybe just a passing shower. 'Jesus,' you said.
'Do you always have to be so... so fucking vicious?'

Now, here I was: on my way to see you
despite the way you'd sighed and soon hung up,
desperate to prove Korea was okay, where you wanted to be
when I knew what you really wanted was me.

Outside the strait was full of boats – impossible to tell
where the stars stopped and the water began.

She

SHEEDAE APARTMENTS, SUNCHEON, SOUTH KOREA

Everything was going to be fine.
'I like it,' you said. 'This view is something else
and your apartment's so much bigger than mine!'
You smiled as I showed you round.

With nowhere else to sit we perched on the bed:
'I can be up the top in twenty minutes if I run.
It's a bit like home, being close to the mountain.'
'Yes,' you said, softly.

I didn't mean for us to make love. Afterwards
we lay like two cuts in parallel: 'Come on,' you said.
'Take me out. I want to see how you live, your city.'
We were just friends, you knew that.

'Or we could just stay here?'
'Come on,' you said again, smiling.

He

McCARTHY'S BAR, JORE-DONG, SUNCHEON, SOUTH KOREA

What were you thinking to take me there? Where expats shoaled
under smoke, twisted to see who this girl was, quite new, with you?
The thought of it flushed my cheek. Was it to show your ease?
How you could cut the crowd, knew everyone?

The bar was a joke. Full of imported stone and horse-brass,
bevelled glass and Guinness, the D-class kind you get
in every 'Irish' pub. Maybe, I thought,
it reminded you of home and looked around the room.

But you weren't there. Minutes passed, growing until I got up
and searched the corridor. Beyond the concrete beaded with sweat
there were street lights shimmering and the sound of a woman
crying somewhere overhead. I looked up –

on the floor above was a woman in tears.
Your hand was on her cheek, the other held her waist.

She

SHEEDAE APARTMENTS, SUNCHEON, SOUTH KOREA

Eventually we stopped and silence came.
I, you, we had nothing more to say, knew
the when, where and she of it better
than any childhood tune.

Outside, dawn played pink notes above the city.
I lay my head on your lap, said
'I don't know what I'm doing,' over and over
until you kissed me, 'Just to shut you up.'

You stayed for two more terrible days.
I slept with my phone under my pillow,
Yoon-mi texting, you in my arms,
both of you furious.

At the airport you asked me, 'Do you love her?'
I answered, 'Not yet.'

He

和歌山
The Poem Mountain
Winter

Shrine

apartments

Mount Jogye

BUSAN →

McCARTHY'S BAR

DONG-CHEON RIVER

Station

54

TEMPLE LODGING, KOYA-SAN, WAKAYAMA, JAPAN

'I would have punched him in the balls,' Kristen said. Spinning
through the turnstile, matching her ticket to the platform board.
'Well, we're going to be friends,' I replied, for who could know
what the future held as you did your thing and I did mine.

In the courtyard, gravel crunched underfoot, shone like a riverbed
where mist dripped off the black willows, darkened the blonde thatch
where we stood and stacked our boots in the yellow genkan.
It had taken way too long to get here: rush-hour delays in Osaka

and now the monk they'd tasked to greet us kept shooting us
little looks, his pen scratching our names in meticulous katakana,
not meeting our eyes in the hall where he took our money on a plate
with a bow. So much faffing. I threw my pack onto my bed.

It puffed like a fungus, full of airborne mildew,
dust motes catching fire in the lamp.

She

SHARKY'S BAR AND GRILL, HAEUNDAE BEACH, BUSAN, SOUTH KOREA

'You know your dick's bigger than anything they've ever had
so you literally just *blam* and they love it.'
It was last minute, this weekend away with the boys in Busan,
spending the first days of summer on the beach.

The girl's apartment smelt like incense and beer,
her breath like toothpaste as we sweated it out on her sheets.
Everyone did it. One guy even hired a whore, found her hand
inside his pocket and chased her down the street.

But now it was Sunday and time for the lads' post-match
analyses. 'Yeah, mate, come on.' 'Tell us what went on.'
Truth was, the next day I wound up helping her. Fetched
boxes for her ma who worked a stall way down in Dong.

How do I always get so involved? I thought
as our glasses chinked and the bubbles dissolved.

He

TEMPLE LODGING, KOYA-SAN, WAKAYAMA, JAPAN

Naturally hot, the water slid over me,
collecting in black pools on the bathroom floor.
I soaked each limb in turn: my large thighs,
let the soap obscure my arms malleable as putty.

'Why don't you have a bath if you've nothing nice to say?'
Kristen had said. The sound of blue gas and monk-chant ran
like a comb over my nerves. 'Just remember, this isn't Korea
and I'm not the one you're angry with.'

The water made bubbles as I prayed, 'I will do anything, *anything*
to get him back –' But I couldn't finish the bargain,
hugged my knees and begged the heat to enter, whispering
'Please, please, please –' hoping God would know what I did not.

Outside, crows called out across the darkening grey.
Their caws circled the redwoods, settled on the water.

She

THE BOSESONG TEA FIELDS, SOUTH KOREA

The night before, we did it in a love-hotel close by.
The snow melted on her eyelashes, soaked into the floor
of yellow matting by the door we didn't have time
to close. I pulled her tight till her body became a bow

arching away from me. Crows woke us rooting for scraps,
drew me to the thin crack of curtain light falling
across the bed. I imagined how it must feel to live as light:
splitting the dark, a pure lapse through a window.

But we had plantations to see: snow-covered shrubs
and the tea tips lemon-grey in the intermittent sun.
In the tea-house, she ordered for us both,
set the water to bubble over a small flame.

'Watch,' Yoon-mi commanded, as the leaves
unspooled: gunpowder grey into brilliant white.

He

OKUIN CEMETERY, KOYA-SAN, WAKAYAMA, JAPAN

The incense was inside the rain. Cinnamon, camphor,
aloeswood and amber bled between the graves,
circled the gated sarcophagi and the stone mausoleums.
Redwoods disappeared above the fog-thatch. The wind slid

down the branches, stirred banks of moss and the roots gnarling
their whiteness into the soft, black mulch. Kristen took my hand,
pulled me through the graves back to the path with its slight camber
caused by a millennium of pilgrims. 'Come on, we'll miss it.'

They held the ceremony deep within the inner walls.
Beyond the bowls of incense and the purple sweep of monk robes
we sat cross-legged on the rush floor surrounded by gold,
lacquer boxes, brass lilies and sweet potatoes framing the Buddha.

It should have been beautiful. I should have been moved –
I closed my eyes, felt nothing but black.

She

SHEEDAE APARTMENTS, SUNCHEON, SOUTH KOREA

Your voice had not been to sleep. I heard
the watching inside it draw back, across
the Sea of Japan, the Sea of Korea, curling
voices and distance like prayer scrolls.

 'You can't not talk to me forever,' I said.
I heard the particular click of binary
that was your breath: you were on the edge,
half turned-away and the wanting of you thrilled me.

'Fine,' you said. 'Let's talk.' But that
was too much, already. Smelled like attack
to me, already faithless, shouldering
off the dirt like it was dark and clotted panic.

Why did you always get to be so sad?
Your surrenders like a weapon descending.

He

TEMPLE LODGING, KOYA-SAN, WAKAYAMA, JAPAN

Max told me once that just before a pilot breaks
the barrier of sound he goes temporarily deaf. I lay
watching dawn lighten the paper panes, reaching
for the sound of rain I knew was falling, couldn't hear.

He knew a lot about Japan, that friend. If a friend
is really what he was. He told me about temple gardens,
how beyond the raked zen stones you'd find bamboo and bonsai
kept in the dark, Jizo-gods with moulded bibs.

For all their shadowy neglect those gardens still flourished:
toadstools, ferns, a special kind of dog daisy that opens
when the light ascends an octave over twilight.
Things can grow even when you don't want them

but how much of that growing comes from faith,
how much from a lack of options?

She

SHEEDAE APARTMENTS, SUNCHEON, SOUTH KOREA

And then, one day, I let Yoon-mi choose
the music. Through sex and sleep, guitar punctured:
cracked falsetto and the backwoods
sound of Bon Iver blasted huge as a warehouse.

She put on our music: mine and yours.
I felt my lungs' each branch and bend humming
like a panicked bird. Our intimacies,
each fragility, and still Yoon-mi cranked the sound.

But then she kissed me and I was diving down
to Warrenpoint again, green paint peeling
and the sharp, salt tang of water, only
this time I didn't care enough to hold back.

'One more in a long line of sad shags,' I thought,
winded, lying on my back.

He

PACIFIC APARTMENTS, JONAN-DORI, HIROSHIMA

'I think I might have been a bit deluded,' I said, as Kristen
sat beside me on the bathroom floor, letting her hand trail
in the water. 'You wouldn't be the first,' she said, frowning,
swirling the white suds round and round the tub.

'Deep down I felt so sure, still feel he'll turn up and surprise me.
Did I ever tell you he always knew where I was?' I asked,
rubbing a line of bubbles from my lip, 'Yes, babe, you did.'
I gave up and let my shoulders sink into the water.

Kristen sat quietly with me while I cried. When I was done
she took the towel she was warming and wrapped me in it.
She dried my hair, she helped me with my buttons, she lay beside me,
our bodies two question marks watching the neon sky.

All the ceilings of my life had clattered through my guts.
'Lord,' I prayed, 'make me strong enough to give him up.'

63

She

ROYAL HOST RESTAURANT, JONAN-DORI, HIROSHIMA, JAPAN

All along the river-path lanterns bobbed in the trees.
They encircled an oyster bar, the water reflecting neon and stars.
Downtown, in ramen and gyoza shops I searched for you.
It took all night until finally I asked a white dude –

'Do you know where the Royal Host restaurant is?'
Back across the overpass, by a bicycle park the orange sign glowed.
There were Zelkova trees, flower beds, neat tram tracks
in parallel and balconies like a climbing wall running up the road.

It seemed so simple: book the flight, board the plane
and find you. I'd managed to hitch
my way to the city. I waited for the lights to change
then crossed, trying to figure out which block was yours.

It didn't take very long. Less than the hour it took you
to open your door to me. Knocking, begging, knocking again.

He

Part Three
City of Rivers
Years Later

PAASEIG DE MERLA, VALLDOREIX, SPAIN

Back then, I believed the things I'd done made me bad.
It pissed me off. I wasn't the first person to break
a heart. I know people who do it all the time and it costs
them nothing. Yet I was lumbered and it dragged me down.

Problem was, for every inch of life I gained back there you were.
'If only I could grow beyond,' 'If I could get him back.' The fantasy
of saying no obsessed me. That has been the final challenge:
to not want more, to try and keep this soft peace pure.

But sometimes, when I'm jogging past twelve on an autumn night
and mist pillows up the river and the mountains are listening —
when the stars overhead blink like angry diamonds I'm sure I've got it right,
even as the wind shears the world of leaves and I run to keep from freezing.

I'm not afraid to take these river paths that get so lost in mist,
I keep going and smile: jaw set, clenching my fists.

She

LISHEEGAN FARM, BALLYMONEY, NORTHERN IRELAND

We still see each other maybe once every two years.
I'll schedule a layover when it isn't needed
or she'll drive miles out of her way to stop in for tea
when my wife's away, on holiday with the kids.

'Remember when you ate that oxo cube
off my palm?' she'll ask, supressing a grin.
Stirring the grey leaves from years ago I keep
on a high shelf no one can reach in the back kitchen.

But truthfully, we both prefer to meet in public.
Something about crowds, queuing for coffee or at the gate waiting
reminds me of that bible story, how Elizabeth
and the child inside her leapt when they felt Mary nearing.

Something about her eyes,
the intimacy crowds afford us.

He

The End

THANKS

Thank you to all the friends and colleagues who became my family in Hiroshima, especially Ayako Matsumoto, Cristina Toledo, Jennifer Stuart, Kimberley Aono, Whitney Lewis and Nic Dobbins. Thank you to Alice Herring, Amanda Macgregor, Bernadine Nixon and Caroline Cook for oh, everything. Thank you to Ashley Goligher, James Lau, Mark Atkinson, Robert Bamford, Sue May Chung and William Bamford for your friendship and all the fun and love you brought into my life. Thank you to the staff and students of the MSt in Creative Writing at The University of Oxford and to Jane Draycott in particular – having you take my work seriously was a marvel and still is. Thank you to my family for all your love and support, especially to my parents who let me live with them while I wrote this book – thanks for not minding when I ditched the whole lawyer thing. Extra-special thanks to Maria C. Goodson for your friendship and comments on the early drafts of this book and to Hannah Bressler for your creative input but even more importantly, for your love of this story and for helping me to believe in it again. Thank you to Alex P., Rosanna, Todd, Cate, Alex W. and Edwin at Eyewear for loving, editing and publishing this book and for all your kind words and support. Finally, to my husband Paul Austin – you have created the space and time in our life together for my work to happen. Thank you.